ISBN 978-0-266-89654-8
PIBN 10906190

1916 CLASS BOOK

VOLUME I

PUNCHARD HIGH SCHOOL

Andover   -   -   Massachusetts

PUBLISHED BY SENIOR CLASS

THE ANDOVER PRESS
ANDOVER, MASS.

THE PUNCHARD SCHOOL

To our comrade and friend,
Nathan C. Hamblin,
we dedicate this book.

Nathan C. Hamblin

NATHAN C. HAMBLIN, Principal   101 Chestnut Street

Latin·

EUGENE V. LOVELY   141 Main Street

Science

EDNA G. CHAPIN   105 Chestnut Street

LOIS J. REED   48 Elm Street

Business

ELIZABETH M. LOFTUS   105 Chestnut Street

History

RUTH K. WHITING   2 Chestnut Street

Domestic Science

PERCIVAL M. SYMONDS   33 Chestnut Street

Mathematics

MARY L. SMITH   79 Chestnut Street

English

HELEN DeM. DUNN   2 Chestnut Street

French and German

Miss Loftus   Mr. Symonds   Miss Chapin   Mr. Lovely   Miss Smith
Miss Reed   Mr. Hamblin   Miss Whiting   Miss Dunn

Class Book Board

ANN S. LESLIE, *Chairman*

LILLIAN M. McCARTHY   WALTER S. LAWSON

The Senior Class

CORA ELIZABETH ABBOTT

CORA ELIZABETH ABBOTT

"Still achieving, still pursuing."

Goldsmith Prize Speaking, 1914.   Class Gifts

RUTH ELIZABETH ABBOTT
"RUFUS"

"Who gives himself with his gift feeds three."

Lincoln Spelling Match, 1915, First Prize.   Barnard Prize Speaking, 1916, First Prize.   Senior Play.   Essayist.

RUTH ELIZABETH ABBOTT

9

DELIA MAUD BELISLE

DELIA MAUD BELISLE
"DAHLIA"

"The girl who laughs, heaven bless her."

First Prize in Botany, 1914.   Class Statistician.

GERTRUDE WELLS BERRY

GERTRUDE WELLS BERRY

"A voice so soft, gentle and low."

First Latin Prize, 1913.   Barnard Prize Speaking, 1915, Second Prize.
Barnard Prize Speaking, 1916, Second Prize.   Vice-President.   Senior
Play.   Valedictorian.

AUGUSTINE EDWIN BROWN

"He doth nothing but frown."

Baseball; Captain in 1916. Football. Treasurer Class. Senior Play.

AUGUSTINE EDWIN BROWN

MADELINE MARGUERITE FITZGERALD

"MAUDIE"

"Your heart's desires be with you."

MADELINE MARGUERITE FITZGERALD

11

ANNA MARGARET HARNEDY

ANNA MARGARET HARNED[1]
"She gazed — she reddened like a rose."
Goldsmith Prize Speaking, 1915. Senior Play. Class Prophet.

CATHERINE LOUISE HICKEY
"CATH"
"But still her tongue ran on."
Lincoln Spelling Match, 1916, Second Prize.

12

CATHERINE LOUISE HICKEY

AGNES BLANCHE HIGGINS

"Is she not passing fair?"

Goldsmith Prize Speaking, 1912, 1913.

AGNES BLANCHE HIGGINS

ELDRED WILSON LARKIN

"LARKY"

"Nor is the wide world ignorant of his worth."

Baseball; Captain in 1915. Football. Goldsmith Prize Speaking, 1914, First Prize. Barnard Prize Speaking, 1915, First Prize. Class President. Editor-in-Chief of *Ensign* 1915-1916. Senior Play. Class Historian.

ELDRED WILSON LARKIN

WALTER SCOTT LAWSON

WALTER SCOTT LAWSON
"YUGGA"

"Let me not burst in ignorance."

Football; Captain in 1915. Baseball. Class Book ·Board. President of Athletic Association.

ANN STRACHAN LESLIE

ANN STRACHAN LESLIE

"Oh, that laugh of thine will cause thee trouble yet."

Ensign Board. Class Book Board. Senior Play. Salutatorian.

14

LILLIAN MARGUERITE McCARTHY

LILLIAN MARGUERITE McCARTHY
"SNOW"
"Drink to me only with thine eyes."
Senior Play.   Class Book Board.

PEARL MARGARET McCOLLUM
"LADY"
"Friends, 'tis the hour to sing."

PEARL MARGARET McCOLLUM

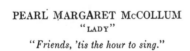

JOSEPH WILLIAM McNALLY

JOSEPH WILLIAM McNALLY
"JEFF"

"Let me have men about me that are fat."

Baseball. Barnard Prize Speaking, 1915. Senior Play. Class Will.

JOHN DUFTON NOYES
"JOHNNIE"

"Soft! Who comes here?"

Football. Goldsmith Prize Speaking, 1915. Manager of Baseball Team, 1916. Barnard Prize Speaking, 1916. Business Manager of Senior Play.

JOHN DUFTON NOYES

16

ISABELLE STAFFORD PETERS
"PETE"

"Then let thy love be younger than thyself."

Glee Club

ISABELLE STAFFORD PETERS

GLADYS ELISABETH RALPH
"RALPHIE"

"Her face is fair, her heart is true."

Senior Play

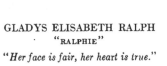

GLADYS ELISABETH RALPH

17

WILLIAM JOSEPH RILEY
"BILL"

"Your mind is tossing on the ocean."

Baseball.   Football.

WILLIAM JOSEPH RILEY

JENNY ROSELINE WETTERBERG
"JEN"

"A daughter of the gods, divinely fair and most divinely tall."

JENNY ROSELINE WETTERBERG

18

PAULINE FRANCES WOOD

PAULINE FRANCES WOOD
"JOE"
"*As merry as the day is long.*"

SARAH LEVINA WOODHEAD
"SADIE"
"*Thou shalt not know the sound of thine own tongue.*"
Second Latin Prize, 1913. Essayist.

SARAH LEVINA WOODHEAD

GUY WEBSTER

GUY WEBSTER

" Then he will talk — good gods! how he will talk."

Football   Baseball

Class Song

I

Here, Classmates, side by side we stand,
At life's broad, open shore,
Resolved that '16 noblest be
Today and evermore;
In all, both earnest work and play,
Uphold the Gold and Blue;
Dear Punchard, to thy name alway
Be loyal, firm and true.

II

For thee, fair Alma Mater,
And for our classmates all
We'll faithfully strive onward,
Where'er life may us call.
Now as we leave thy halls so dear,
We pledge our love to thee;
Within our hearts thy name revere
To all eternity.

ISABELLE PETERS

21

Class History

HE entrance of the Class of 1916 into the Punchard School, like our departure therefrom, was accompanied by a wave of excitement that swept over the whole country. We came here just as people were beginning to cheer themselves hoarse for Taft or Roosevelt or Wilson and we leave while shouts of exultation or groans of disapproval are still echoing from two great national conventions.

The fact, however, that 1912 was a campaign year was of only minor importance to us. The change of administration in which we were most interested was the one that came with our promotion to a new school. The question that troubled us was, "What will these powers that be do to us?"

We soon found out. We were first divided into two unequal parts and distributed over Room 2 with its dull and dreary interior and Room 5 with its noisy seats.

Then began the struggle with x, y, z, and *amo, amas, amat*. Some of our number appeared to be struggling with unknown quantities and with the same distracted verb. The chief events of our Freshman year were football, baseball, and the Goldsmith. We were represented in the Goldsmith Prize Speaking by Miss Blanche Higgins and William Foster. On the football team, three of our class represented us and on the baseball team we were represented by four men. Miss Gertrude Berry secured the first Latin prize for the Freshmen class and Sarah Woodhead obtained the second honors.

At the beginning of our Sophomore year most of us found ourselves hermetically sealed in Room 4, where we attacked our weighty problems with renewed vigor and among our achievements was the mastering of Caesar. The Geometry was felled by our constant corrosion of its "roots", and French and English were readily absorbed by our mental powers.

23

Miss Blanche Higgins and Eldred Larkin were chosen to represent us in the Goldsmith. Seven of our class made the football team and three made the baseball nine. Miss Delia Belisle was awarded the first prize in botany.

In our third year most of us again went into cold storage in Room 4, while a few of us were allowed the privilege of being entombed with the Seniors in the dungeon darkness of Room 6. In the case of one of our members the cold of Room 4 "struck in". The brain of Lawson appeared to congeal and he was constantly found wandering, in a dazed condition, through the corridors. At last, Miss Whiting took pity on him and from that time on through the year he followed her about like Mary's "little lamb".

In the Goldsmith, Miss Cora Abbott and Eldred Larkin represented the Class and the latter was awarded the boy's prize. In the Barnard Prize Speaking Contest, the essays of Miss Gertrude Berry and Eldred Larkin were chosen by the judges for the finals in the Town Hall. Eldred Larkin captured the first prize and Miss Gertrude Berry the second. The football team included five of our class and the baseball team had four of our members in its lineup.

Our class tendered a reception in the form of a truck-ride to Canobie Lake, to the Seniors, and a jolly time was had by all.

Last September those of us who had survived the rigors of a winter in Room 4, joined the advance guard in Room 6. Goggles now became more in evidence, adding to the learned aspect which we had acquired through three years of violent mental activity. A notable addition to our class was made in the person of one "Dinnis O'Hara", otherwise known as McNally.

Six of our members made the football team and five made the baseball nine. Miss Anna Harnedy and John Noyes represented us in the Goldsmith. Miss Gertrude Berry, Miss Ruth Abbott and John Noyes were chosen for the finals in the Barnard Prize Speaking Contest. Miss Abbott was awarded first prize and Miss Berry won the second prize. A

24

reception by the Juniors was given us in the November Club House and we were very pleasingly entertained.

We have held parties at frequent intervals at the homes of different members of our class this spring and these will long be remembered by us as one of the most pleasant features of our high school career. The Class gave a play in the Town Hall to raise funds for the class gift and it was a great success in every way.

Now as we leave the halls of dear old Punchard and our path separates, we cannot help hesitating on the threshold to ponder over our situation.

While most people are interested in the results of the great conventions at Chicago and St. Louis, we are most concerned in the results of our departure from Punchard and the effect it will have on the community and on ourselves.

Class Prophecy

A reunion was called for the Class of 1916 in the year 1936 and I was delegated to look up our graduates. Living down in China at the time, I thought that since I had not seen the "Old Town" for nineteen years, I would come. But did I see the old town? No, indeed; it had grown to be a flourishing city with great stores, theatres and even aeroplanes. Not seeing anyone I knew, I decided to aeroplane to the "Phillips Inn" and dispose of my grip. When I was seated comfortably, I began to feel uneasy about my classmates. To my great astonishment I spied Pete Tyler, a little gray-haired man, of three feet six inches, running the aeroplane. Of course Pete had to tend right to business and had no time to talk. However, he told me that he was still keeping bachelor's quarters and had not been away from Andover since he was graduated. I also learned that Gladys Ralph was employed in his Aeroplane Company as his time-keeper.

At last, I reached my destination and instead of finding what I had supposed to be the "Phillips Inn", I found a very beautiful hotel. On stepping into the office to register, whom should I see but my old friend, Isabelle Peters, the proprietress of the establishment. Poor Isabelle had been so unfortunate as to marry only twice, and losing both of her husbands was obliged to make her own living. After she had told me all her troubles, I informed her of my errand and you may rest assured she was a mine of information.

Of course, I was given a beautiful room and, being very tired, went to bed early. The next morning while reading the *World's News*, I discovered a fine article on the European war of 1914, written by Gertrude Berry who had won international fame as an historian.

My trunk had not arrived and, having been invited to go to the opera with some friends, I journeyed down town and went into one of the large department stores to purchase an evening gown. The manager directed me to the latest Paris styles on the fifth floor. Seeing

26

an interesting gown on one of the models, I went very close to examine it. There with all her girlish beauty stood Madeline Fitzgerald, who greeted me warmly and fitted me out with a stunning gown.

Isabelle had told me that Larkin was performing in the Stock Company at the theatre, and as we had some time to wait, we stepped in, just in time to see Larkin rush upon the stage to the accompaniment of soft music, and rescue the heroine, Cora Abbott, from the trapeze upon which she was performing.

As we left the theatre an attendant offered us some handbills announcing that Ann Leslie would deliver a stereopticon lecture on the following evening. She was still with the Merrimack Mutual Company and was touring the country giving talks to large audiences on Insurance.

The bill also announced that the Cosmopolitan Quartet from Buenos Aires consisting of Webster, Brown, Lawson and McNally, would make their appearance on the following week.

While we were waiting for the aeroplane, we saw an illuminated electric sign which bore these words:

BEAUTY PARLORS, TRANSFORMATION WHILE YOU WAIT
LILLIAN M. McCARTHY

DIMPLES EXECUTED WITHOUT PAIN
PEARL M. McCOLLUM

As I stepped into the elevator, I heard the shrill voice of Blanche Higgins. Blanche, clothed all in yellow, was trying to convince the clerk that because she was the leader of the "Women's Rights Movement", she should have the best room in the hotel.

27

There were so many things to do and to say, I deferred my return to China till the following month.

Being anxious to renew acquaintances we decided to hold our reunion the next week at Isabelle's hotel. Notices were immediately sent out and a telegram was received from Catherine Hickey, the great cabaret dancer, at the Hippodrome in New York, stating that she would be present at the reunion to give us an exhibition of modern dances.

The next day we journeyed to see the Health Exhibit which was being held in Mechanics Building. We were met by Jenny Wetterberg who, with the help of a megaphone, was inviting people to come in. She directed us to the cereal table, where we found Sarah Woodhead. She had been traveling through Massachusetts as a drummer for the "Shredded Pine Needle Biscuit Company" and had built up a large business.

Tired but elated at seeing so many classmates, we were about to return to Andover when we noticed a large poster bearing the words, "*Thousands die every year from poor milk.*" In going over to investigate we beheld John Noyes demonstrating for the "Noyes Evaporated Milk Company".

He informed us that Bill Riley was possessed of the world's goods and held the responsible position of Chairman of the Chicago Produce Exchange. He represented his Company at the exhibit and planned on spending a few days in Ballardvale before resuming his duties again.

Having a few minutes to spare before our train left, we walked slowly down Washington Street, and noticed a familiar figure rushing towards us. It was that of Ruth Abbott, who looked very prosperous. Of course I was prompted to ask her if the world had treated her well, though had I thought seriously I should have surmised that Ruth early developed the gift of speech and was now singing the praises of the Roller Roller Talking Machine.

Returning to Andover, we immediately began our preparations for the coming event. Suddenly a thought came to me of Delia Belisle,— what of her? After a course in nursing, she went to France to care for wounded soldiers. Her love for the French and the fluency with which she spoke the language soon endeared her to a French officer, and now at our twentieth reunion, I find her a devoted citizen of France

The last member of the glorious class to be heard from was Pauline Wood. After graduation she studied very seriously and became a professor in Brown University.

The night of the reunion came and as we gathered round the festive board we rejoiced that Time had not robbed us of any of our members. To add to the joy of the occasion Mr. Hamblin surprised us by his presence. He motored up from Oklahoma, having left the care of the State University in other hands.

Soon after I departed for San Francisco en route for China, with a new spirit of gladness and with a deeper feeling of love for Andover, Punchard, and for each and every member of the dear old Class of 1916.

ANNA M. HARNEDY

Alphabet

A is for Ann, a demure little lass,
B is for Blanche, liveliest one in our class.

C stands for Cora who is moderate, not quick.
D is for Delia, a regular brick.

E stands for Eldred, an Artistic Scream,
F for Fitzgerald who thinks she's a dream.

G is for Gertrude who cannot be beat,
H stands for Harnedy, ever smiling and sweet.

I is for Isabelle whose feet are immense,
J stands for Jenny who sometimes lacks sense.

K is for Katherine who talks all the time,
L stands for Lillian, a charmer sublime.

M for McNally, a would-be sport,
N stands for Noyes who is summoned to "court".

O is for order; Room 6 has its share,
P stands for Pearl with her nose in the air.

Punchard 1916

Q by necessity must be left out,
R is for Ralph who can flirt, there's no doubt.

S stands for Sarah who lives by rule,
T is for Theodore, thin enough to keep cool.

U I'll take out and substitute I,
   Perhaps you may guess the reason why.

V is for volleys you'll fire by and by,
W is for Webster who thinks he's some "Guy".

Senior Book Shelf

CORA ABBOTT	*A Maid All Forlorn*	ANN LESLIE	*Anybody but Ann*
RUTH ABBOTT	*How She Raves*	LILLIAN MCCARTHY	*Secretary of Frivolous Affairs*
DELIA BELISLE	*A Good-Hearted Girl*	PEARL MCCOLLUM	*Wanted — A Chaperone*
GERTRUDE BERRY	*The Cyclopedia of Education*	JOSEPH MCNALLY	*Master of Silence*
GUS BROWN	*Out of Step*	JOHN NOYES	*Down on the Farm*
MADELINE FITZGERALD	*She Would if She Could*	ISABELLE PETERS	*It*
ANNA HARNEDY	*Innocents Abroad*	GLADYS RALPH	*Cupid's Understudy*
CATHERINE HICKEY	*Bunch of Yarns and Rare Bits of Humor*	WILLIAM RILEY	*Happy-go-lucky*
ELDRED LARKIN	*The Boss*	JENNY WETTERBERG	*Wanted — A Hero*
WALTER LAWSON	*A Victim of Good Luck*	PAULINE WOOD	*The Eternal Laughter*
SARAH WOODHEAD	*What's in a Name?*		

32

DRAMATICS

The Rebellion of Mrs. Barclay

JUNE 9, 1916

MORTON BARCLAY	Eldred Larkin
ETHEL BARCLAY, *his wife*	Gertrude Berry
MARY ANN O'CONNOR	Anna Harnedy
RUTH CARTER, *Ethel's sister*	Ann Leslie
ELSIE STUART, *a neighbor*	Lillian McCarthy
MRS. BROWN, *Morton's sister*	Ruth Abbott
CORA, *her daughter*	Gladys Ralph
ROGER STUART, *Elsie's brother*	Augustus Brown
DENNIS O'HARA	Joseph McNally

ACT. I — The Dining-room at the Barclays'
ACT II — (Five days later) The kitchen
Prompter — BLANCHE HIGGINS
Business Manager — JOHN NOYES

33

Ensign Board

EDITOR-IN-CHIEF -	ELDRED LARKIN
BUSINESS MANAGER - -	WILLIAM BREWSTER
SCHOOL NEWS EDITOR - - -	ANN LESLIE
ATHLETIC EDITOR - - - -	EVERETT HATCH
SUBSCRIPTION AGENT -	GEORGE KNIPE

ATHLETICS

Webster Adams E. V. Lovely, Coach Eastwood Boutwell H. Larkin H. Brown Watson Crosby, Manager W. Cronin
Holt Morrill G. Abbott Geo. Brown
Noyes Riley Lawson, Captain A. Brown E. Larkin

Football

Shortly after school opened in the fall of 1915, Mr. Lovely, the coach, issued a call for football candidates and about thirty men reported for practice. The candidates worked hard for two weeks and opened the season in an auspicious manner by defeating the Sanborn Seminary eleven by the overwhelming score of 53 to 0, on the Playstead.

Next the Punchard eleven journeyed to Derry, N. H., where they played a scoreless tie with the Pinkerton Academy team of that town in a bitterly fought contest.

On the 12th of October, our team romped home victorious by a score of 24 to 0 against Methuen.

Punchard again took the measure of the Sanborn Seminary boys on the 19th of October by the score of 46 to 0.

Our first defeat came on October 22, when Pinkerton Academy came down from Derry, N. H., and trimmed us to the tune of 13 to 7.

On October 30, we were again taken into camp, this time by the Beverly Industrial School, by the score of 13 to 6.

For the second time, the Punchard eleven defeated the Methuen team by the score of 19 to 7.

On Saturday, November 20, we defeated our old rival, Exeter High, at Exeter, in the annual game, by the score of 13 to 6. We had the heavier team but the Exeter lads fought hard throughout the contest and forced us to exert ourselves to the limit in order to win. The first touchdown was scored by Punchard in the second period, when Captain Lawson crossed the goal on an end around play from the 25-yard line. H. Larkin kicked the goal. Exeter scored in the third period on a forward pass but failed to kick the goal. We scored our second touchdown in the last period when E. Larkin shot a forward pass to Cronin from the 20-yard line. At the end of the game Punchard had the ball on Exeter's 2-yard line.

BASEBALL

Baseball

Punchard opened the baseball season by defeating the Alumni by the overwhelming score of 15 to 7. Our team played good ball considering that it was the first game of the year.

The next game was at Wakefield and the Punchard boys came through victorious by the score of 13 to 0.

On April 25, the Punchard nine played a sensational game with the Lawrence High School team which went twelve innings to a 4 to 4 score.

Next the Wakefield team came to Andover for a return game and was again defeated, this time by the score of 12 to 4.

On May 12, we journeyed to Derry, N. H., where we received a trouncing to the tune of 21 to 11. Both teams played poor ball in this game but Punchard's misplays came at critical moments, with disastrous results.

We received our second defeat at the hands of Reading on May 19, at Andover. The contest was slow and many errors cost us the game.

The next day we played and defeated the Danvers High School nine on Brothers Field, by the score of 7 to 5, in an interesting game.

On May 26, we got sweet revenge on Pinkerton when we turned the tables on them by winning with the score of 13 to 6.

The Methuen team were our guests on the Playstead May 31 and we had a lively time with them, finally sending them home on the short end of a 16 to 15 score.

At Reading on June 2 a close and exciting game resulted in a victory for Punchard, 3 to 2, while on the following day a ten inning contest was won from Danvers at Danvers, the final score being 4 to 3.

Lawrence cancelled its second game and the Exeter contest was postponed to June 14, on account of rain. Stoneham was defeated on the Playstead, Tuesday, June 13, in a closely played game by an 11 to 9 score.

The following day at Exeter our hopes for a fitting finish to a successful season were shattered for Exeter won easily 12 to 1.

GRINDS

Grinds

We like our German, "Miss Dunn is so kind,
And if we forget things, why, she doesn't mind'
She merely corrects us and starts us anew,—
I wish other teachers were like that, don't you?

Lord Percy has a happy way
Of making things so very clear,
That only on the brightest day
Can they be seen at all, I fear.

Miss Chapin practices the art
Of keeping perfect quiet;
And she succeeds so well, I wish
That others too would try it.

In caverns neath the Samuel J.
There is a land of empty shelves,
Where sits a sorcerer every day,
And teaches Physics to his elves.

Miss Smith is so kind-hearted,
She hopes our tales are true.
If they are not too extravagant,
She'll stretch a point or two.

On Wednesday should a smell arise,
Oh, conjure not what it may mean;
'Tis but Domestic Science C,
Which burneth incense to its Queen.

To sections of the Sophomore class
Miss Reed doth make a daily trip,
To help their puny, infant hands
To launch a Penman-ship.

We pity Mr. Hamblin for the work he has to do
In the very narrow confines of his little four-by-two:
With one leg in the doorway and the other doubled tight.
If no one's sharpening pencils, there is room enough to write.

Miss Loftus runs our school affairs
With hand that cannot fail;
And though Ford cars are selling cheap,
Our "Lizzy's" not for sale.

Lightning Source UK Ltd.
Milton Keynes UK
UKHW020915220119
335965UK00013B/1832/P